3/95

BODIES IN CRISIS

HEREDITARY DISEASES

Jacqueline L. Harris

Twenty-First Century Books

A Division of Henry Holt and Company
New York

Twenty-First Century Books
A Division of Henry Holt and Company, Inc.
115 West 18th Street
New York, New York 10011

Henry Holt® and colophon are registered trademarks of Henry Holt and
Company, Inc.
Publishers since 1866

Published in Canada by Fitzhenry & Whiteside Ltd.
195 Allstate Parkway, Markham, Ontario L3R 4T8

Printed in Mexico
All first editions are printed on acid-free paper.

Created and produced in association with Blackbirch Graphics, Inc.

Library of Congress Cataloging-in-Publication Data

Harris, Jacqueline L.
      Hereditary diseases / Jacqueline L. Harris. — 1st. ed.
           p.   cm. — (Bodies in crisis)
      Includes bibliographical references and index.
      Summary: Discusses heredity and how genes function as well as the types,
symptoms, and treatment of hereditary disease.
      ISBN 0-8050-2603-7 (acid-free paper)
      1. Genetic disorders—Juvenile literature. [1. Genetic disorders. 2. Diseases.]
I. Title. II. Series.
      RB155.5.H37 1993
      616'.042—dc20
                                                                93-25913
                                                                CIP
                                                                AC

Contents

Genetic material passed on by parents to children determines the children's physical and biological traits.

1

Chromosomes and Genes: The Materials of Heredity

Heredity refers to the passing on of characteristics to children. These passed-on, or inherited, characteristics may be physical traits, such as having blue eyes or being tall. They may also be disorders, which can cause a variety of problems, as in the following cases:

• A baby is born with a malignant tumor in its eye. Without treatment, the baby will surely die as the tumor spreads to other parts of its body.

• A 36-year-old woman develops twitching in her face, arms, and legs. Nerves deep in her brain are slowly destroyed, and she eventually dies.

• A man drives right through a red light because he can't see the color red. If he is hit by another car, he may be fatally injured.

All of these people's problems, which were inherited from their parents, began deep in the cells of their bodies. Cells are the tiny roundish or oval structures that make up all forms of life. Body cells have two parts—the nucleus and the surrounding fluid, or cytoplasm.

Inside the nucleus of the cell are tiny, tightly coiled threads called chromosomes. Chromosomes are made of a chemical that directs the development, growth, and function of all life—in trees, ants, bears, flowers, bacteria, and people.

Each cell in the human body, except for the reproductive (sex) cells, has 23 pairs of chromosomes, or 46 chromosomes. The reproductive cells have half the number of chromosomes. Chromosomes are inherited from our parents. The human body begins to form when the father's sex cell, or sperm, unites with the mother's sex cell, or egg, to form a fertilized egg. Since the sperm and the egg have 23 chromosomes each, the fertilized egg winds up with a total of 46 chromosomes.

Through a complex process, this fertilized egg eventually produces trillions of cells to form a new life. If this process has gone on as it should have, each cell in the body of the newborn baby, like that of the parents, will contain 23 pairs of chromosomes. Half of these 46 chromosomes come from the mother, and half come from the father. In this way, parents pass on to their children eye color, blood type, body type, and all of the other physical characteristics that the child will have.

Chromosomes act in pairs. Half of the chromosome pair that carries the message for eye color, for example, comes from each parent. Together, these two chromosomes determine the child's eye color. Thus, a father who has blue eyes may not necessarily have a child

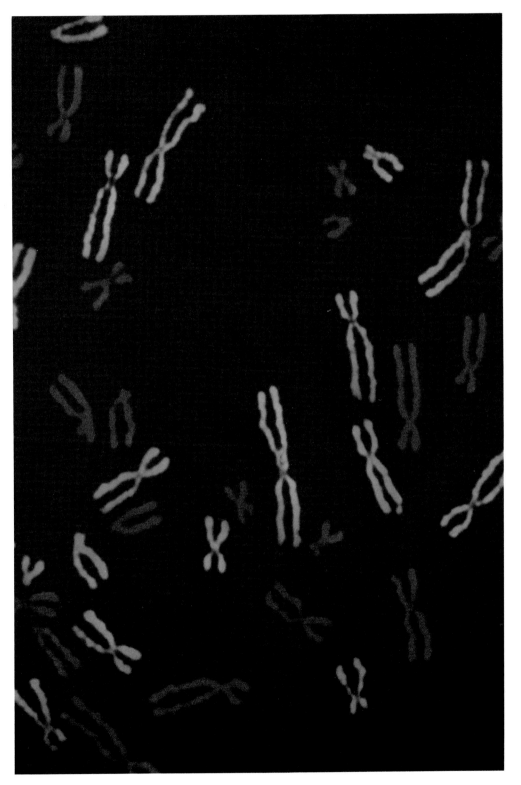

A computer-color-enhanced photograph shows a grouping of human chromosomes. Every cell in the human body—except the sex cells—contains 46 chromosomes. Each kind of chromosome, arranged in a specific order, controls a particular genetic trait.

with blue eyes. The color of the child's eyes depends on how the mother's chromosome for eye color interacts with the father's chromosome for eye color.

Chromosomes can be identified under a microscope by their size and the arrangement of the dark bands across their width. Scientists have numbered them 1 through 23. Chromosome pairs 1–22 direct the development and functioning of the body. Scientists know that each pair has many different jobs. One pair, for example, directs the formation of a chemical used to digest starch. That same chromosome pair also directs the formation of some of the proteins that make up a person's blood type. But scientists do not yet know all the roles of each pair of chromosomes.

The twenty-third pair, called the sex chromosomes, controls the sex of a baby, as well as other traits. There are two kinds of sex chromosomes—X and Y. A developing baby with two X chromosomes will be a female. A male will have an X and a Y chromosome.

Arranged in pairs along the length of each chromosome are 50,000 to 100,000 genes. Genes are the parts of the chromosome that determine the characteristics, or traits, passed on by parents to children. Everyone inherits two genes for a particular trait—one gene from the mother and one from the father.

Genes play many roles. Some are operator genes, controlling the actions of other genes. Regulator genes, in turn, direct operator genes. Architectural genes control the overall structure of the body, such as the length of the fingers and the location of the ears.

All human physical characteristics are a direct result of genes inherited from our parents. How we look—from hair and eye color to height and weight—has been directly influenced by the genes received from our parents when the body's cells were just beginning to multiply.

Chromosomes and Genes

A GENE MAP

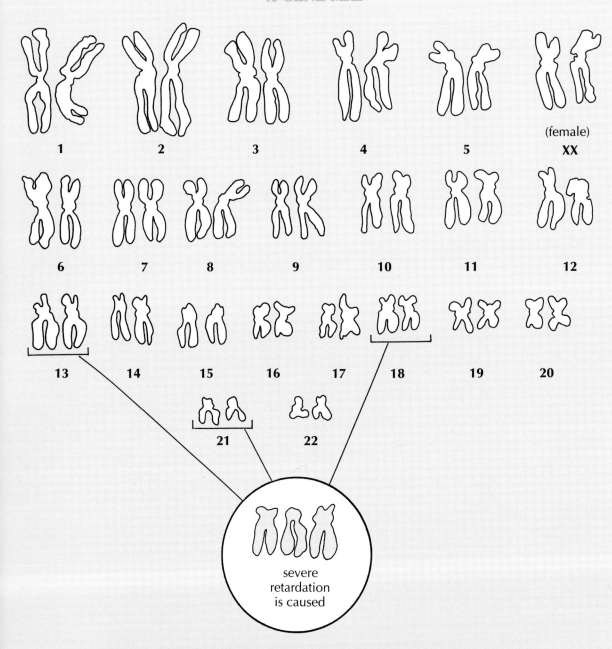

Scientists study chromosomes and genes by looking at chromosomes in pairs and in a special order. This is called a gene map. Each pair—part of a distinct human sequence—controls a certain aspect of the body. When an extra chromosome is attached to pairs 13, 18, or 21, for example, severe mental retardation occurs. The abnormality that is caused by an extra chromosome 21 is called Down syndrome.

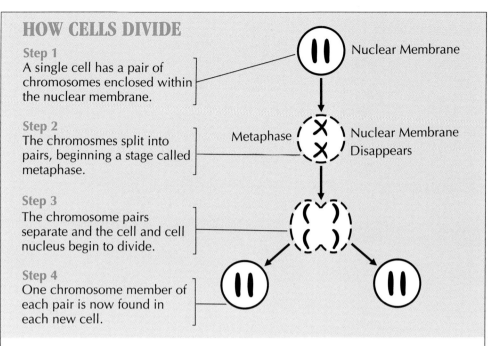

HOW CELLS DIVIDE

Step 1
A single cell has a pair of chromosomes enclosed within the nuclear membrane.

Nuclear Membrane

Step 2
The chromosmes split into pairs, beginning a stage called metaphase.

Metaphase

Nuclear Membrane Disappears

Step 3
The chromosome pairs separate and the cell and cell nucleus begin to divide.

Step 4
One chromosome member of each pair is now found in each new cell.

Genes accomplish their jobs by making proteins. Some proteins form parts of the body. Others control body functions, such as digestion or movement.

This chapter has explained the normal functioning of genes. But when something goes wrong—a needed protein is not made, too much of a certain protein is made, or an architectural gene is defective—the person will have an inherited disorder. For example, if one protein essential for the clotting of blood is not made properly, the person will bleed a lot even from a minor cut. That person has a disorder called hemophilia.

The following chapters will describe hereditary disorders, explaining what can go wrong with chromosomes and genes and the effects that are produced by defective chromosomes and genes. The last chapter discusses exciting new methods being used to cure and treat hereditary disorders.

A child with Down syndrome waits for a playmate in a swing. Down syndrome—caused by an extra chromosome in pair 21— is one of many hereditary diseases caused by malformation of the chromosomes within the body's cells.

2

When Chromosomes Are Damaged

Sue was very happy when she discovered that she was going to have a baby. She and Bill had been married for three years and wanted to have a lot of children. But, two months after she learned that she was pregnant, Sue began to have stomach cramps. Then she began to bleed. The blood was coming from her vagina—the opening in the body that leads to the uterus, where babies develop before they are born.

At the hospital, the doctor told Sue she was having a miscarriage. She was losing her baby. The fetus was tearing away from its attachment to her uterus. It was too small to live outside Sue's body. Later, the doctor examined the body of the baby. He found an abnormal chromosome. Sue's body had probably detected this defect and rejected the baby. Nearly 50 percent of all miscarriages are caused by a defective chromosome. Some babies with a defective chromosome are carried by the mother through the full nine months of pregnancy and are born normally. But their defective chromosome can cause serious physical problems at some point later in their lives.

What happens to chromosomes? During the process of cell formation, a cell divides into two cells called daughter cells, and the chromosome splits down its length. (This occurs about 50 billion times during a person's lifetime.) Sometimes this chromosome split isn't perfect. If a chromosome fails to split during cell division, one of its daughter cells will have an extra chromosome. The other cell will lack that chromosome. Chromosomes may break, lose sections, or have their parts rearranged during their split. A defective chromosome in a liver cell, for example, may cause problems for that organ. But defective chromosomes in the sperm or the egg may be passed on to an embryo (developing baby). The person developing from the embryo will have that defective chromosome in all its cells. Depending on the kind of defect, the person may have a hereditary disorder.

Extra Chromosomes

An extra chromosome also carries an extra set of genes. Scientists believe that excess protein produced by these genes causes hereditary disorders.

A child born with an extra chromosome 21 is said to have Down syndrome. Children who have Down syndrome have serious mental and physical problems.

They are retarded, which means their intelligence is low. They are short, they have flat faces with slanted eyes, and their hands are short and broad. They may also have heart and intestinal disorders and hearing defects. At about age 30, someone who has Down syndrome may begin to resemble an elderly person. Until recently, most children with Down syndrome did not survive beyond the teen years because of the other birth defects that often accompany the disorder. Today, advancements in medicine have extended life expectancy, and constant education and environmental stimulation have allowed them to make the most of their capabilities.

Two disorders similar to Down syndrome, but less common, are caused by an extra chromosome 13 and an extra chromosome 18. Children with these disorders, which produce severe retardation and physical defects, usually do not survive their fifth year.

Chromosome Breakage

Sometimes a chromosome may break into several pieces during its lengthwise splitting. The pieces may move around and attach upside down. This is called chromosome inversion. Chromosome inversion changes the location of the genes on the chromosome. Location is frequently important for the way the genes work. Depending on the chromosome, chromosome inversion can cause such conditions as severe retardation, heart disease, and brain defects. The heart disease can be treated with surgery, but little can be done for persons with mental retardation and brain defects.

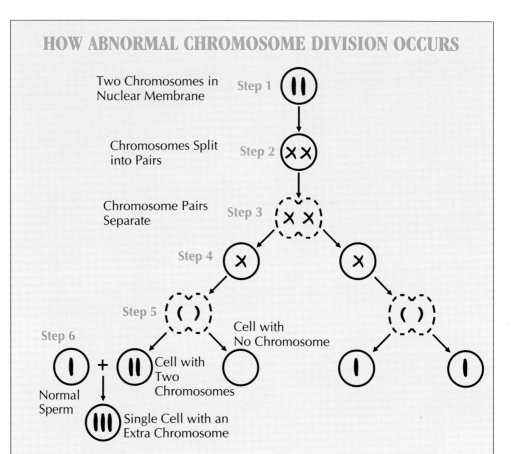

HOW ABNORMAL CHROMOSOME DIVISION OCCURS

Two Chromosomes in Nuclear Membrane — Step 1

Chromosomes Split into Pairs — Step 2

Chromosome Pairs Separate — Step 3

Step 4

Step 5

Step 6

Cell with No Chromosome

Cell with Two Chromosomes

Normal Sperm

Single Cell with an Extra Chromosome

Sometimes when a chromosome breaks, a piece of it may be lost. If this occurs along a certain part of chromosome 5, the child will be born with a condition called cri du chat (cry of the cat) syndrome. The baby has a narrow throat, making its cry sound like that of a cat and causing difficulty in swallowing. Its face is very round, and its eyes are far apart. Afflicted with heart problems and retardation, the child usually does not live beyond two years.

Chromosome breaks are also responsible for many kinds of cancer. The loss of a piece from chromosome 13 causes a child to be born with a tumor in the retina of its eye. Early treatment with chemicals and X rays can prevent the cancer from spreading to the rest of the body. Usually if one of the parents has a history of this problem in his or her family, the doctor will check the baby for a tumor after birth.

Wilm's tumor, a kidney cancer, occurs when a piece is lost from chromosome 11. It mainly affects children and is treatable.

Sex-Chromosome Abnormalities

Chromosomes 23 are the sex chromosomes, X and Y. Normal males are born with one X chromosome and one Y chromosome. Normal females are born with two X chromosomes. An extra sex chromosome in the male or female or the lack of one can cause severe hereditary disorders.

Males In general, males who are born with an extra X chromosome do not show signs of having a problem until they are teenagers and start developing breasts. Males with this defect have small testes (male sex glands) that do not make sperm, meaning they can never father a child, and they lack other male characteristics. They are also very tall and have abnormal bones. Often mentally ill, they can have difficulty getting along with others. Many are retarded and have learning problems. Treatment with special body chemicals called hormones reduces the size of the breasts, makes the voice deeper, encourages the growth of hair on the face, and makes the penis slightly larger. This enables them to have normal sex lives.

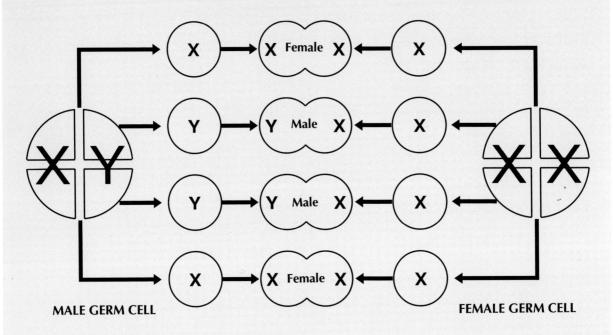

MALE GERM CELL   **FEMALE GERM CELL**

Male germ cells have one X and one Y chromosome. Female germ cells have two X chromosomes. When the four sex cells are formed from the male cell, they combine with four from the female cell. The resulting combinations create two possible females (XX) and two possible males (XY).

Males born with an extra Y chromosome may have learning disabilities. Such males are usually very tall and suffer from a severe skin condition that leaves pock marks on the face and upper body. Some scientists have tried to link extra Y chromosomes with criminal behavior, but no link has been shown to exist.

Females Females born with three X chromosomes may be very tall, may have small heads, and may have some learning disorders. They have problems with menstruation (monthly period), but most lead normal sex lives and have normal children.

Females with only one X chromosome, however, can suffer more serious problems that do not usually show up until they are teenagers. They are very short, lack breasts, have webbed necks (folds of skin extending from neck to head), short fingers and toes, bulging eyes, and small chins. While their intelligence is normal, they sometimes have trouble learning. Some may suffer from thin bones, deafness, heart disease, high blood pressure, kidney disease, and crossed eyes. These problems can all be treated. Most females with this chromosome defect lack ovaries—the sex glands that make eggs—and cannot bear children. Treatment with hormones encourages the growth of breasts and other sex characteristics.

Males/Females Some babies may be born with a fragile X chromosome. A certain point on the fragile X chromosome breaks, damaging the gene.

A fragile X chromosome is found mostly in males. It is the cause of about one fourth of all mental retardation in males and is the most common inherited cause of mental retardation among the entire population. It also affects their nerves, facial structure, testes, skin, heart, muscles, and bones.

Females may also have this chromosome defect, but the effects are much less severe than in males. About one third of females with this condition may be mildly retarded, have some facial problems, and have ovaries that are abnormally large.

When Chromosomes Are Damaged

A computer-enhanced photograph of a DNA chain shows the basic connections that make up the chemicals in genes. DNA and RNA are both nucleic acids and are important elements in all genetic material.

Genes That Don't Work Properly

3

When Janie was born, she seemed to be a happy, healthy baby. But when she was three months old, she started having seizures during which she twitched and jerked uncontrollably. Her parents also noticed that Janie had an unpleasant smell, sort of musty and dirty. She developed a skin rash. The doctor said that Janie had a disorder called phenylketonuria (PKU) that caused a chemical to accumulate in her body. The chemical would eventually damage her brain and some bones unless she was put on a special low-protein diet.

Janie's problem had been caused by one defective gene. The gene is supposed to make a protein that dissolves the chemical that was building up in Janie's body. The chemical is found in most protein. A low-protein diet with milk substitutes relieves the symptoms.

Most babies are screened at birth for this condition. This disorder is one of about 4,000 caused by a defective gene. How can one tiny structure cause so many problems? If you know how genes work, it is easier to understand.

Understanding Genes

As was explained in Chapter 1, genes control the body's structure and function by making proteins. Proteins are used to form parts of the body or to perform certain jobs. Sometimes the proteins trigger other genes to act. Each human cell contains all of the genes that control the structure and functions of the body. But some genes in different body cells are "switched off." If they weren't, people would have teeth growing on their legs and hair growing in their stomachs. Only those genes needed by the cells to form the organ or perform the function of that organ are "switched on."

Amino acids Chromosomes are divided into genes, which are small segments of chromosomes. These genes are made up of a chemical called DNA, which is, in turn, made up of nucleic acids. These nucleic acids come in four different types and band together like colored beads on a string. Each group of three nucleic acids is called a codon. Each codon makes up a certain amino acid. These acids are linked to form the 20,000 different proteins that the body needs. Each gene's codons are strung together in a particular order. The codons direct the production of amino acids in order, and the chain of amino acids then forms the correct

The "Father" of Genetics: Gregor Mendel

The first person to discover the existence of genes and to formulate a theory of heredity was an Austrian monk named Gregor Mendel. Working alone in a monastery garden, Mendel did experiments with pea plants. He crossbred different varieties of peas and observed what resulted. When new plants grew, Mendel would study a few of their basic characteristics, including plant height, seed color, seed shape, pod shape, pod color, and flower distribution. After each crossbreeding, Mendel took careful and detailed notes, describing the physical characteristics that developed in each plant.

In 1865, Mendel reported his findings to the Brunn Natural History Society in Austria. It was there that he first told other scientists about his theories of heredity.

Mendel said that during the formation of the sex cells (the egg and sperm), factors for certain traits in genes separated. This meant, for example, that a sperm or an egg could contain a factor for either tallness or shortness but not both. This theory was called Mendel's first law.

Mendel also stated a theory of dominance in genes. This was based on the idea that each inherited characteristic is the result of an interaction between two hereditary factors (one gene from each parent). Some characteristics, Mendel observed, always dominated over others. If one of the chromosomes, for example, contained one gene for tallness and one for shortness, the offspring would always exhibit tallness. This meant that the gene for tallness was dominant over the gene for shortness.

The significance of Mendel's work was not completely realized until after his death. By 1900, however, other scientists had expanded Mendel's research and used his findings to lay the foundation for the development of modern genetic theory.

protein. But if even one of those codons is changed, the wrong amino acid is made, thus producing the wrong protein. The wrong protein or the lack of the correct protein causes the hereditary disorder. A person might lack the proper protein needed to form normal skin. Perhaps he or she lacks the protein needed to control another gene.

Mutations Changes to gene codons are known as mutations. Certain chemicals can cause mutations. Mutations can also be caused by intense energy called radiation. The sun, the center of the earth, and certain man-made devices such as X-ray machines and nuclear reactors used in electric-power plants produce radiation. It is not known how chemicals and radiation produce mutations. Mutations are also believed to be simply variations that occur during cell formation.

If a mutation occurs in a body cell such as a liver cell, the person may begin to have problems with his or her liver. But if the mutation takes place in a cell in the sex organs, the person's eggs or sperm will carry the defective gene. The child who develops from that cell with a defective gene may develop a hereditary disorder.

Dominant and recessive genes There is a pair of genes for every kind of protein made. Each pair is for a specific trait. Whether a child is affected by a single gene depends on how the two genes, one from each parent, act together. In some cases, such as hair color, one gene may make the protein for dark hair. The other may make the protein for blond hair. The dark-hair gene, which will always overpower the effects of a blond-hair gene, is said to be *dominant.* If a child has one dark-hair and one blond-hair gene, he or she will have dark hair. If both of the child's hair-color genes are for blond hair, the child will have blond hair. The gene for blond hair is said to be *recessive.*

About 2,000 hereditary disorders are caused by dominant genes. If the dominant gene of the pair of genes is flawed, the person will have the disorder.

Recessive genes cause about 1,400 disorders. If the person has one flawed recessive and one normal

Certain physical traits, such as hair and eye color, can express themselves differently in each member of a family, depending upon how the genes from each parent first combined.

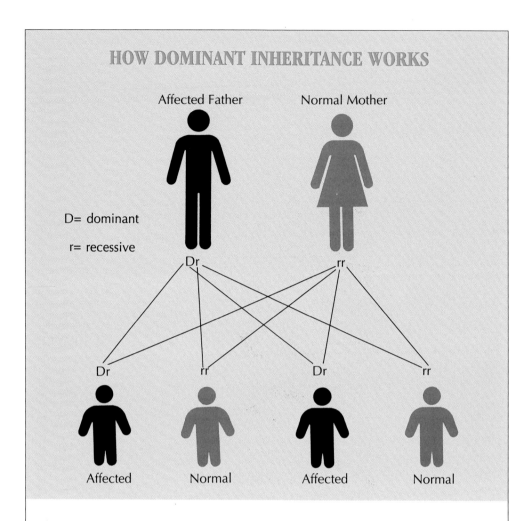

HOW DOMINANT INHERITANCE WORKS

Affected Father

Normal Mother

D= dominant

r= recessive

Dr

rr

Dr

rr

Dr

rr

Affected

Normal

Affected

Normal

recessive gene, he or she won't have the disorder but may have slight symptoms of the disorder. While the flawed gene is making the wrong protein, the person seems to get enough of the needed protein from the normal recessive gene. But if both recessive genes are defective, then the person has a hereditary disorder.

Dominant-Gene Disorders

Some of the many disorders caused by dominant genes that are defective, such as Huntington's chorea, are rare.

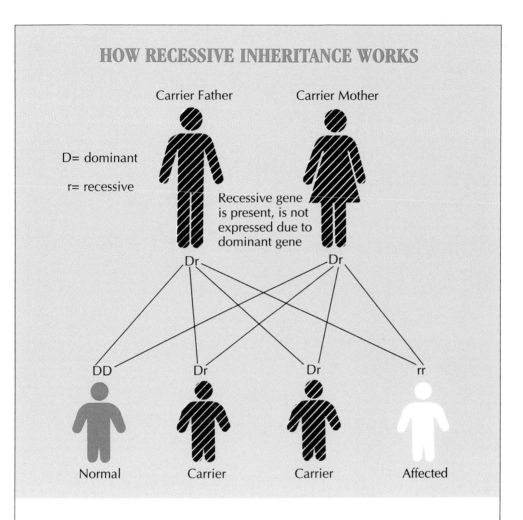

HOW RECESSIVE INHERITANCE WORKS

Carrier Father   Carrier Mother

D= dominant

r= recessive

Recessive gene
is present, is not
expressed due to
dominant gene

Dr   Dr

DD   Dr   Dr   rr

Normal   Carrier   Carrier   Affected

Atherosclerosis, on the other hand, is one of the most
common hereditary diseases.

Huntington's chorea This disease is believed to be
caused by a defective gene on chromosome 4. It is the
result of the gradual destruction of brain cells, which,
unlike other cells, can't be replaced. The first symptoms, which don't appear until 30 or 40 years of age,
are twitches and clumsiness. Gradually, victims begin to
make meaningless movements. The body twists and
turns, and facial expressions constantly change. These

Dwarfism is a hereditary disease that prevents proper bone growth in the arms and legs.

uncontrollable movements make it hard for victims to speak, to use their arms and hands, and to walk. Remembering and thinking become difficult. Through it all, affected people are completely aware of all these problems, which causes much emotional pain. As a result, many victims become mentally ill, and some try to kill themselves.

Doctors can do very little except try to lessen the uncontrollable movements. Gradually, the person loses the ability to walk and talk. Death occurs after about 15 or 20 years. Studies of the brains of those who have died from Huntington's chorea show a large hole where brain cells have been destroyed by the disease.

Dwarfism Most people who are abnormally short (dwarfs) have a disorder in which the ends of certain bones in their arms and legs do not grow properly. As a result, the person has very short arms and legs and waddles when walking. Dwarfs also most often have large heads, but normal intelligence. Since it is dominant, dwarfism occurs when one of a pair of genes is flawed. A child born with two dwarfism genes will have serious bone abnormalities that will prevent the normal functioning of the lungs and the brain. The child will die by the time he or she is several months old.

Atherosclerosis Atherosclerosis is a disease of the arteries—the vessels that carry blood from the heart to the body. Fats in the blood collect on the arterial walls. As a result, the openings of the arteries become narrow, sometimes closing entirely. This is a particular problem for the small arteries that supply the heart. When these

ALS and MS: Still Searching for the Answers

Amyotrophic lateral sclerosis (ALS) and multiple sclerosis (MS) are two diseases that affect the nervous system. *Sclerosis* is the general medical term for the hardening of a body tissue.

MS is a significant disease in America, affecting anywhere from 5 to 30 people per 100,000 (depending upon geographic location). As the disease slowly destroys nerve fibers, the nerves in the body lose their ability to function properly. The common symptoms of MS include lack of coordination, weakness, blurred or unclear vision, and numbness in various parts of the body.

ALS is similar to MS in that it, too, is a disease of the nervous system. With ALS, cells in the brain and the spinal cord are destroyed—these are the areas that control movement in the body. As these cells (also called motor neurons) are lost, muscular weakness and eventual paralysis usually follow. Because baseball legend Lou Gehrig was one of the first people known to suffer from ALS, the disease has also become commonly known as Lou Gehrig's disease.

The causes of ALS and MS are not known, but many researchers and scientists believe that heredity and environment may play a part in these diseases. Because a significant number of cases seem to occur in families that have been previously affected, scientists are studying the hereditary links and causes carefully. One recent breakthrough in the research on ALS has been the identification of a gene that makes some families susceptible to the disease. Having identified this gene, doctors are hopeful that they will be able to find effective treatments for ALS.

arteries narrow or become entirely blocked, the heart does not receive the oxygen and food carried by the blood. The muscles of the heart cannot move properly, which interferes with the heart's job of moving blood through the body. The person has a heart attack.

Atherosclerosis occurs mostly because people inherit the tendency to make too much of several kinds of fat in their blood. Some fats pose great risks to the heart. Others cause diabetes, high blood pressure, and obesity (excessive weight). High levels of fat in the blood can be treated with medicines and diet. Patients are also advised not to smoke or drink alcohol.

Recessive-Gene Disorders

Some disorders caused by defective recessive genes more commonly affect members of specific racial or ethnic groups. That is because ethnic groups and races share a gene pool with each other that is more closely related on the average. People who have European-Jewish or French-Canadian ancestry, for example, are the most likely to inherit Tay-Sachs, a brain disorder. The incidence of the blood disorder sickle-cell anemia, on the other hand, is found almost exclusively in African-American populations. Cystic fibrosis, a respiratory disease, is the most common hereditary disorder among white populations of European lineage. Following is additional information on each of these ethnic-based diseases.

Tay-Sachs This disorder is caused when a pair of defective genes fails to make the protein that controls the amount of certain fats in the brain. The fat collects in the brain, gradually destroying the brain cells. Babies born with Tay-Sachs seems normal until they are about three or four months old. Then they start to become less active. They stop crawling, playing, smiling, and making sounds, and they lose the ability to sit up or use their arms. Breathing and swallowing become very difficult, and the babies become blind and deaf. Propped up on pillows, such babies lie motionless, staring into space. They usually die of pneumonia between two and five years of age.

Scientists have identified the protein that Tay-Sachs victims lack, but they do not know how to get it into the

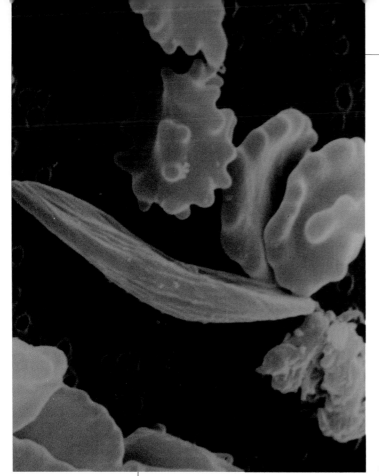

A microscopic close-up of a sickled cell surrounded by normal, round blood cells. Sickle-cell anemia is a blood disorder caused by a defect in a gene in chromosome pair 11.

brain, where it is needed. There is no treatment for Tay-Sachs disease.

Sickle-cell anemia A serious blood disease, sickle-cell anemia is caused by a flawed gene located on chromosome 11 that produces a defective form of a protein called hemoglobin. Blood carries oxygen from the lungs to all parts of the body. It is the hemoglobin inside the donut-shaped red blood cells that transports the oxygen. Hemoglobin combines with the oxygen, releasing it when it is needed. The problem for the person with sickle-cell anemia is that the red blood cells change shape when the oxygen is released. The release of oxygen causes the sickle hemoglobin molecule to change shape. As a result, the red blood cells become sickled, or spearlike, in shape. This sickled cell clogs the blood vessels, cutting off circulation. The lack of blood circulation and the short life of sickled red-blood cells decrease the amount of oxygen supplied to the body. This oxygen starvation causes the symptoms: pain in the joints and abdomen, ulcers and sores on the legs, and dizziness and fatigue caused by a weakened heart.

If the person is chilled or tired or gets an infection, his or her body has an increased need for oxygen. Many red blood cells will release oxygen and become sickle-shaped. The person then has what is called a sickle-cell crisis. In the crisis, the person suffers severe pain in the back, stomach, arms, and legs. Joints swell and hurt. The bones, heart, lungs, and kidneys may be damaged by the severe lack of oxygen brought on by the blocked blood vessels. Doctors treat sickle-cell crises with oxygen, blood transfusions, medicines for the pain, and lots of liquids. Lack of liquids can also cause red blood cells to become sickle-shaped.

Cystic fibrosis This disease is the result of a defective gene on chromosome 7. The normal gene produces a protein that moves salt and water in and out of the cells of the lungs, sweat glands, pancreas (an organ near the liver that makes digestive juices), and the intestines. These organs produce mucus, a thin, sticky liquid that bathes the tissues, washing away disease organisms and harmful substances. If the cells of those organs lack that important protein because the gene is defective, they produce very thick mucus. This thick mucus interferes with the functioning of these important organs and will eventually begin to damage them.

The symptoms of the disorder begin during the first months of life. The baby has one cold after another, which may be followed by serious lung infections such as bronchitis or pneumonia. The child is thin and produces a greasy, smelly bowel movement. The mucus also clogs the lungs, making breathing difficult. Disease

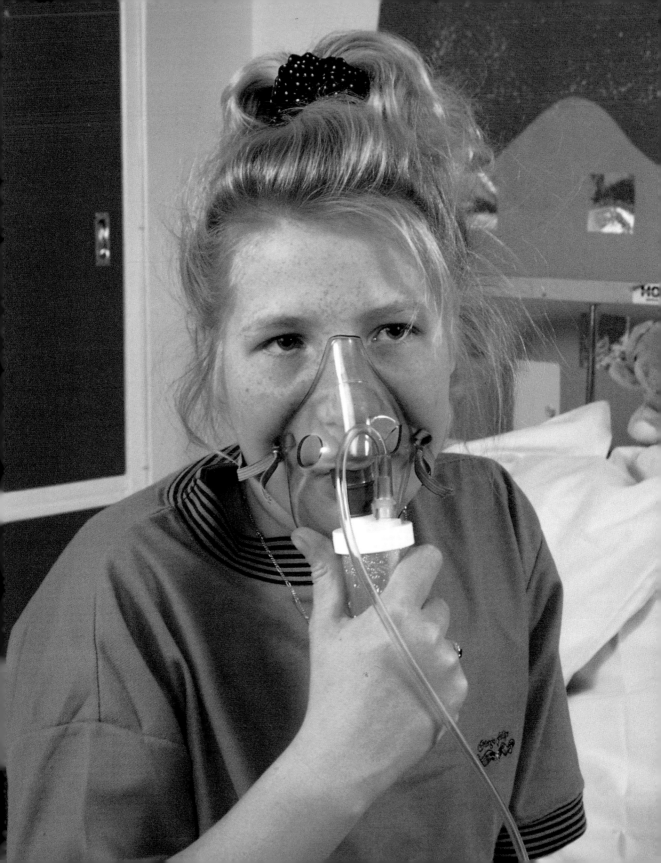

organisms multiply in the mucus, which causes lung infections. Mucus blocks the passageways in the pancreas so that the digestive juices cannot flow into the intestine, where most food digestion takes place. Thus the food the person eats goes right through the body. The sweat glands release large amounts of salt in the sweat. Losing so much salt can severely affect the body and even cause death. The thick mucus may also affect the testes, preventing the release of sperm. Thus a male who has cystic fibrosis usually cannot father children. Cystic fibrosis is such a serious disease that females dare not risk pregnancy. Pregnancy could worsen the disease and cause a heart attack or diabetes.

Treatment reduces the effects of the mucus. Several times during the day, cystic-fibrosis victims must have their back repeatedly clapped with the palm of a hand. This procedure loosens the mucus in the lungs so it can be coughed up. Cystic-fibrosis victims also take antibiotics (medicines that prevent or kill infection). Pancreatic digestive proteins are added to their food to help digestion. Since they do not absorb the vitamins from food well, cystic-fibrosis victims must take vitamin supplements. The typical cystic-fibrosis victim may take 50 pills a day. In the 1950s, cystic-fibrosis victims usually died by age 5. Today they can live to their late twenties. This life expectancy may be further extended as a result of new medicines being tested. One of these medicines dissolves the mucus in the lungs. Another medicine helps the body transport salt and water in and out of its cells.

Two of a Kind: Identical Twins

Although it happens relatively rarely, some mothers give birth to more than one child at the same time. Because multiple births are uncommon, they offer researchers and scientists special opportunities to study the environmental and hereditary factors that influence the development of children.

Many different kinds of multiple births are possible. When two babies are created from two separate fertilized eggs and each of them has a different genetic makeup, they are called fraternal twins. Identical twins, on the other hand, are formed from a single fertilized egg that separates into two different embryos. Identical twins are always the same sex, they always look exactly like each other, and they frequently behave in similar ways. Why do they have all these similarities? Because their genetic makeup is identical.

Two or more people with exactly the same genes are of particular interest to genetics researchers. Because it is known that the chemical and biological factors of identical twins are identical, scientists can better evaluate the effects of the "outside" influences, such as child-rearing, diet, and schooling. Important studies have been done on identical twins, and some of the research has proven to be very interesting. Several of these studies have shown that identical twins raised separately in completely different places still share an unusual similarity in intelligence and personality. Is this just coincidence, or do your genes really determine your intelligence and what your personality will be? The final answers are still to be found.

X-Linked Disorders

X-linked disorders are those in which the defective gene is carried on the X chromosome. As explained earlier, a female has two X chromosomes, while a male has one. It is important to remember that in recessive-gene inheritance, the person will not have the disorder if one gene of the pair of genes is normal. The normal gene makes up for the harmful effects of the defective one. Thus, if a baby girl inherits one X chromosome with a defective gene and one normal X chromosome, she will not have the disorder. But a boy who inherits an X chromosome with a defective gene will not have another matching gene to make up for the defective one—his other sex chromosome is a Y. He will therefore get the disorder. A baby girl who inherits two X chromosomes with the defective gene will also get the disorder. There are about 250 X-linked disorders. A few of these disorders are described here.

Hemophilia Hemophilia is a blood disorder in which the person lacks one of the proteins that make blood clot. Bleeding caused by an injury continues for a long time. This bleeding can be very dangerous if it occurs in the brain or the joints, since the pressure of the blood damages these important body parts. People with hemophilia—almost always males—can be treated with injections of the clotting protein that their bodies lack. Even though hemophilia is the most common bleeding disorder, it is still a very rare disease. Only about 1 male in 10,000 is born with hemophilia.

Color blindness A flaw in the eye's retina (the light-sensitive coating on the back of the eye) causes color blindness. As a result, the affected person cannot see the colors red and green and

Certain hereditary disorders are said to be X-linked because they are caused by a defective gene that is carried on the X chromosome. Hemophilia, for example, is an X-linked disorder that prevents blood from clotting.

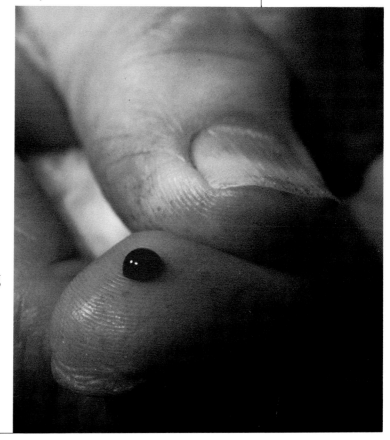

Look at the colored circle below. What do you see? If you are a female, you probably see the number 32 in the center of the circle. If you are a male, however, you may not see anything at all.

The inability to see the colors red, green, blue-violet, or some combination of these is an inherited trait called color blindness. The severity of color blindness varies from individual to individual and most commonly affects color perception only mildly.

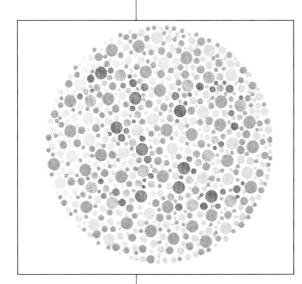

Color blindness is almost always a hereditary disorder. The defect is transmitted on the X-chromosome, which contains the genes that determine the male sex characteristics. This means that color blindness is found almost exclusively among the male population. Approximately 8 percent of all males have some form of color blindness, while a mere 0.44 percent of women are somewhat color-impaired.

Color-blind people are at a great disadvantage in certain situations. In operating a motor vehicle, for example, color-blind people must pay extra attention to traffic signals. Many of these people can tell the difference between "stop" and "go" on a traffic light only by the position of the glowing light—not the color. Certain branches of the armed forces will not accept people who are color-blind, and some occupations—mostly involving visual design—are simply not practical for color-blind individuals.

sometimes blue. True color blindness, in which a person sees the world in shades of black, white, and gray, is extremely rare. Most color-blind people are males, but women may carry the defective gene and pass the defect on to some of their children.

Duchenne muscular dystrophy This is the most severe and most common kind of muscular dystrophy, but all forms of muscular dystrophy are rare. It affects males only—about 1 or 2 in every 10,000 boys inherit the disease. Muscle fibers all over the body are slowly destroyed. The symptoms begin when the person is very young. The child sits up and walks much later than a normal child. When children with Duchenne muscular dystrophy do begin to walk, they waddle and have trouble climbing stairs. By the time they are 12, they cannot walk at all. The muscles of their hearts become so damaged during their teenage years that they die of heart attacks.

Mitochondrial Disorders

Very rare conditions, known as mitochondrial disorders, have just recently been discovered. Mitochondria are hot-dog-shaped structures that are located in the area surrounding the nucleus of the cell. They produce the cell's energy and thus act as the cell's power plants. A cell may have hundreds of mitochondria. They are not governed by the genes in the cell's nucleus but have their own genes. If one of those genes becomes defective, the mitochondria cannot function, and the cell loses one of its power plants. Mutations in mitochondria are much more frequent than in the cell genes. Thus a cell can eventually lose a great many power plants. At some point, groups of cells can no longer function because they have no energy. This lack of energy can cause heart attacks, muscle disease, and kidney disease

Little is known about mitochondrial disorders. Many researchers believe that these disorders are recessive, and can be passed on to children by the mother only.

External factors, such as getting anesthesia or taking medication, can bring on the symptoms of certain hereditary diseases.

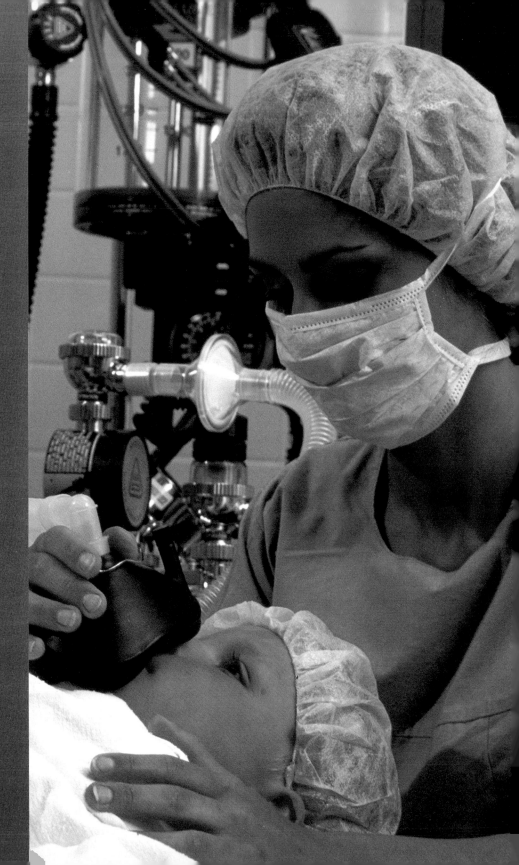

Outside Agents That Bring On Hereditary Diseases

4

It was a simple operation to remove his appendix, but something went terribly wrong as Kenny was coming to after the surgery. His temperature soared to 108°F. His body began to stiffen, and he turned blue. Doctors immediately covered Kenny's body with ice packs. They gave him oxygen and injected medicine into his veins. The doctors' quick action saved Kenny.

Kenny's reaction was brought on by a defective gene that causes a muscle disorder. Under ordinary circumstances, the only effects a person with this disease might experience are mild—droopy eyelids, loose joints, and sometimes weakness in the legs. But the chemical used to put Kenny to sleep before his surgery increased the effect of the gene, causing the severe problems.

There are a number of hereditary disorders like
Kenny's, in which a flawed gene causes a problem when
triggered by an outside agent. That agent can be a
chemical substance such as the one given to Kenny or
just plain aspirin. It can be an infection, factors such as
air pollutants and foods, or things that influenced the
mother while she was carrying her unborn child.

Medicines

Medicines are processed by the body in a certain way.
First the medicine is broken down into chemicals.
These chemicals are carried by the blood to different
parts of the body. The chemicals must then enter the
cells, where they produce the effect the doctor wants—
for example, stopping pain, regulating heart action, or
relaxing muscles. Next, the chemicals are broken down
and eliminated from the body in the urine, in sweat, and
during a bowel movement. There are many steps in this
processing of medicine. Each step is dependent on the
action of a gene. If a gene is defective, however, the
processing is disturbed. Perhaps the medicine, instead
of being broken down and eliminated, builds up in the
body. The high levels of medicine may cause severe
problems. For example, high levels of certain drugs
used to put one to sleep during an operation may cause
paralysis. In other cases, the medicine may be broken
down too fast and may not help the patient.

Many people inherit a defective gene that fails to
make a certain protein needed by red blood cells.
When these people take medicines such as those for

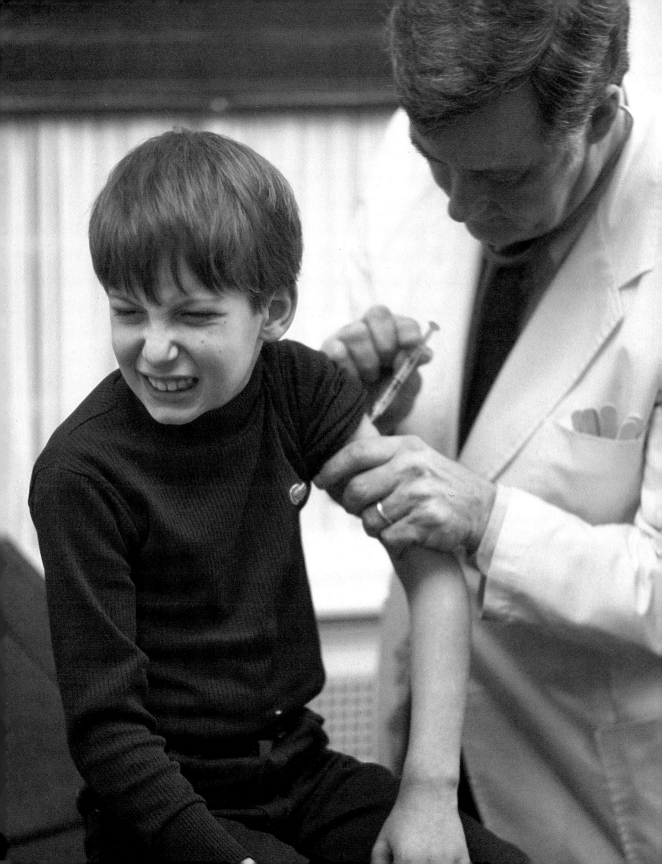

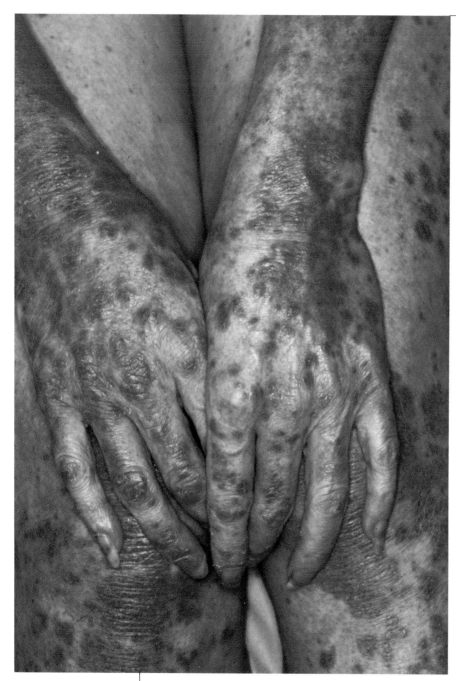

fever, malaria, and pain, their red blood cells break apart. Having lost a number of red blood cells, the person becomes anemic. This means he or she has a lowered ability to carry oxygen to different parts of the body. Not only that, but the contents of the blood cells that have broken apart may move to other areas of the body and cause damage.

Infection

Like medicines, infections can trigger hereditary disorders. Among these disorders are autoimmune diseases and the most serious type of diabetes.

An *autoimmune disease* is one in which the body's immune, or infection-fighting, system turns its defense mechanisms against itself, attacking parts of the body. All the body's cells are covered with a protein coating that protects the cells from the body's immune system, which attacks disease organisms. Production of this coating is controlled by five genes located on chromosome 6. Each of the five genes exists in different forms. Thus there are many combinations that can be inherited. Some put a person at risk of developing an autoimmune disease. An infection is believed to trigger the genes to produce the disease. Among the various autoimmune diseases are several kinds of arthritis (a joint disease), psoriasis (a skin disease), multiple sclerosis (a nerve disease), and two kinds of kidney disease. Autoimmune diseases can be treated with medicines, but these medicines can have serious side effects, including lowered resistance to infection.

Diabetes is a disease of the pancreas, an organ near the liver. The normal pancreas produces a chemical called insulin that regulates the sugar in the body. In a person with diabetes, the pancreas does not work properly, and the body either has no insulin or only small amounts of it. As a result, sugar, the body's important energy source, cannot be used properly. The immediate and most obvious result is lack of energy. Eventually, the affected person may develop problems with blood vessels, the eyes, the kidneys, and the nerves.

There are at least five types of diabetes, two of which are inherited. One, the most serious kind, called

Opposite:
Some individuals inherit a weakness, or a vulnerability, to certain types of diseases. Then, if the conditions are right, they will most likely acquire the disease. Psoriasis is an autoimmune skin disorder that can be brought on by tension, poor diet, and other external factors.

insulin-dependent (type I) diabetes, may be brought on by a viral infection. The person inherits a deficiency in the system that protects the pancreas from infection. Thus, when the person gets a viral infection, the disease organism destroys the cells in the pancreas that make insulin. The infection also stimulates the body to make proteins that destroy the cells of the pancreas. The symptoms, which usually come on suddenly in childhood, are excessive urination, thirst, and hunger; weight loss; tiredness; and angry moods. To prevent these problems, the person takes insulin, which regulates the sugar.

Dietary Factors

For a number of hereditary disorders, food is a triggering factor. Among the foods that bring out these problems are salt, milk products, sugars, fats, and green fruits and vegetables.

High blood pressure has been linked by scientists to a defective gene that fails to govern the water and salt in the body. This condition can cause heart attacks and strokes. It is believed that a diet containing a large amount of salt can worsen the disorder. Doctors can give medicine to lower blood pressure.

Some people, because of their hereditary makeup, can develop diarrhea if they eat milk products. Other people, whose bodies cannot handle certain sugars, can develop liver disease and brain damage and may even die. Those who cannot eat green fruits and vegetables may develop serious nerve damage. And, as discussed earlier, too much fat in the diet can trigger heart disease.

Like other external factors that can trigger hereditary diseases, food and diet can play a large part. High blood pressure, high cholesterol, and digestive disorders are just some of the problems that can be triggered by diet.

The Environment

Environmental factors such as cigarette smoke can bring on certain diseases. One kind of emphysema, a lung disease, is caused by a gene that fails to produce a protein that protects the lungs against poisons. Smoking or breathing polluted air triggers the disease. People with other kinds of emphysema, however, develop the disease from habitual smoking, and not as a result of a defective gene.

Allergies are also triggered by certain elements in the environment. Allergies are physical disorders caused by high sensitivity to foods, substances in the air, or substances that come into contact with the skin. This sensitivity results from a misdirected response of the body's immune system, which is designed to attack invading organisms in the body. The immune systems of people with allergies interpret as dangerous normally harmless organisms—pollen and shellfish, for example. In response to these organisms, the immune system triggers symptoms such as a stuffy nose, a swollen throat, or an itchy rash.

Some people have allergies all their lives, but others outgrow them or develop them as they get older. Being susceptible to allergies seems to have some genetic causes, but there is no evidence that certain genes are responsible for specific allergies.

Developmental Influences

Before birth, the mother's body is the developing baby's environment. Many of the things that happen to the mother can interfere with the development of the baby. During its first three months inside the mother, the baby's heart, liver, eyes, brain, arms, and legs are all forming. It is during this time that environmental factors can do the most harm.

Infection A number of birth defects can be caused during pregnancy if the mother gets certain infections. German measles, for example, can damage the baby's eyes, heart, brain, skin, blood, liver, lungs, and bones. To prevent birth defects caused by German measles, doctors recommend that women who have never had the disease be immunized well before they become pregnant.

Infection by a tiny organism called toxoplasma can also cause severe problems for some unborn babies. The babies may suffer brain disorders that lead to blindness, deafness, and mental retardation. Toxoplasma is found in pet birds and cats, in undercooked pork and lamb, and in the soil.

Among the other infections contracted by a pregnant woman that can damage the unborn baby are chicken pox and sexually transmitted diseases such as herpes and syphilis.

X rays While X rays of the mother usually do not damage the unborn, they have been linked to leukemia (blood cancer) in the child after birth.

Poisons When dumped into waterways, mercury and other factory wastes accumulate in the bodies of fish. Unborn babies are exposed to these poisons when their mothers eat the fish. Mercury can cause severe

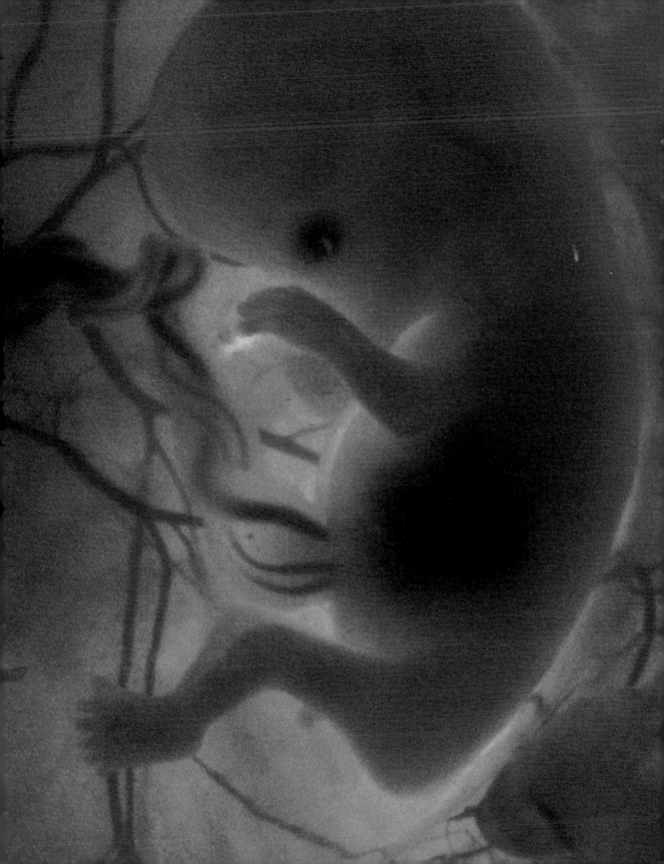

damage to the brain and the body of the unborn baby. Other poisons can cause mental retardation and defects in the skin, nails, and teeth. The unborn baby can also be harmed when the mother breathes in the fumes of chemicals such as gasoline, glue, and hair spray.

Medicines A pregnant woman must be especially careful to follow her doctor's instructions about taking medicine. In particular, medicines prescribed for epilepsy (a brain disorder), heart disease, cancer, acne and psoriasis, and infections can cause birth defects. Even aspirin can be harmful.

Drugs Excessive drinking of alcohol during pregnancy is one of the most common causes of mental retardation in a baby. It may also cause abnormalities of the heart, sex organs, bones, face, and joints.

If a mother smokes, she exposes her unborn baby to the harmful effects of cigarettes, which may cause miscarriage or even death just before or after birth. Babies who survive are often underweight and may develop frequent lung infections and learning problems.

Heroin used by a mother can produce an addicted baby. It may take up to eight weeks for the symptoms of addiction to go away. During this time, the baby twitches, jerks, stiffens up, vomits, runs a fever, develops diarrhea, and sometimes experiences breathing problems.

The unborn baby of a mother who abuses cocaine runs the risk of being born with nutritional and physical problems. The baby may also have serious defects of the eyes, kidneys, bladder, skull, and brain and may develop learning problems.

A researcher works at a genetic-engineering facility in San Francisco, California. Using highly sophisticated equipment, scientists are able to study chromosomes and genes; they can even alter or duplicate them in order to change the biological properties of certain organisms.

5

Cures Are on the Horizon

For all her four years, the little dark-haired girl had suffered from infection after infection. She had been born with a hereditary disorder that crippled her body's immune system, which is composed of proteins called antibodies and two kinds of white blood cells. One kind of white blood cell in the young girl's blood had a defective gene. As a result, the cell failed to make a protective protein needed to fight disease organisms.

On September 14, 1990, as the little girl sat watching television in a Maryland hospital, she was about to make history. She would become the first person to receive gene therapy. Her doctors injected a gray liquid into a vein in her arm. That liquid contained a normal gene that would make the protein that the child's body lacked. Soon blood tests showed that the injected gene was doing its job, making the protein. Gone was the misery of constant infections of the mouth, skin, and throat. Her body was defending itself against infection.

The preparation of the gray liquid that gave the girl immunity was made possible by a great deal of research and knowledge. Scientists had located the defective gene on chromosome 20. By testing normal genes, they discovered the kind of protein that the normal gene made. The goal of the doctors was to put the normal gene inside the girl's disease-fighting white blood cells. This is called genetic engineering.

To accomplish their goal, the doctors needed a natural cell invader. A virus would do the job. Viruses are particles that invade body cells and take over control of the cell. That is how they cause infection. A virus could be used to carry the gene into the girl's white blood cells. Of course, the disease-causing properties of the virus had to be removed.

The doctors needed normal genes that could make the protein. They could get those from normal human white blood cells. The doctors prepared the virus and combined it with the normal gene. They removed a small amount of the girl's own white blood cells from her blood and mixed them with the virus carrying its normal gene. For the next 10 days, the mixture was kept in the laboratory in a warm place. During that time, the virus invaded the white blood cells, delivering the normal gene. The virus, made defective by the scientists, then died. Meanwhile, the white blood cells

multiplied into many millions of cells. Then the gray liquid was injected into the girl's arm.

The white blood cells died after about six weeks (the normal life span of these cells). Since the child could not make new ones, as a normal person would, the girl needed a new injection. But as time passed, she would need injections only twice a year. After investigating ways to get all her body's white blood cells to make the protein, the doctors decided to replace the marrow cells in the center of the sternum (flat chest bone), where new white blood cells are made.

Genetic engineering is now beginning to be tested for use in other hereditary diseases.

Gene Implants for Liver Diseases

A defective gene in certain liver cells causes the body to make too much of the substance cholesterol. The condition, known as high blood cholesterol, can damage the heart, causing heart attacks in children as young as 10.

Scientists have developed a technique in which normal genes are implanted in liver cells. First, nearly one fifth of the patient's liver is removed. Then the liver cells are removed from the tissue. Next, normal genes are inserted into these liver cells by a harmless virus that serves as a messenger. The liver cells containing the new gene are then injected back into the liver by way of a vein that supplies blood to the liver.

This procedure is now being tested on humans. Scientists believe that the protein produced by the normal genes should reduce a patient's blood cholesterol by 50 percent. But the patient would still need other treatment in order to have a normal cholesterol level. The genetic-engineering treatment lasts only until the liver cells die—in about two years, the life span of liver cells. A permanent cure awaits the discovery of the liver's stem cells. These cells produce new liver cells. Inserting a normal gene in stem cells would mean that all new liver cells made by the body would have the normal gene. One treatment would cure the disorder.

Gene Implants for Lung Diseases

Researchers have developed a treatment method for cystic fibrosis that implants normal genes in the victim's diseased lungs. The procedure, effective in laboratory animals, is now being tested on people.

The normal gene is combined with a weakened cold virus. The virus is sprayed into the nose, and the person breathes it into the lungs. The normal gene is carried by the invading virus into the lung cells. In the lungs, the normal gene produces the protein that prevents the buildup of the thick mucus that damages the lungs of cystic-fibrosis victims. The effect would last until the treated lung cells were shed—about two or three months. Then the person would have to use the nose spray again.

Gene Implants for Other Diseases

Gene therapy is also being tested on several kinds of cancers, Duchenne muscular dystrophy, and sickle-cell anemia.

Lung cells, liver cells, and blood cells are easily reached by the doctor. Thus they are readily treated by gene therapy. But hereditary disorders that affect the brain, such as Tay-Sachs, present problems for scientists. They do not know how to implant genes in brain cells safely and effectively.

Making Medicines

Genetic engineering is also being used to make new medicines to treat different kinds of diseases. Normal human genes are implanted in bacteria or yeast. These tiny organisms are grown in laboratory dishes. As they multiply, the organisms produce medicines. These medicines, which are actually proteins made by the normal genes of healthy people, are used to treat sick people. Such medicines include insulin for diabetics, as well as treatments for hemophilia, anemia, and stroke.

This technique is also being used to produce a medicine called human-growth hormone for children who do not grow properly. Now scientists are trying out the technique on cows. The cows would give milk that contained the human-growth hormone.

Genetic Counseling

As scientists working in the field of medical research gain an increased understanding of genetics, technology will enable physicians to provide people with genetic-counseling services. These services are already being offered at a number of major medical centers. This type of counseling helps couples who are concerned about

Scientists are now able to genetically engineer certain viruses, bacteria, and other microorganisms for use in creating medicines. Here, researchers check the progress of a special genetically engineered yeast that will be used to make medicine for people with liver disease.

having children with genetic disorders because of their age or because of a family history of a specific disease. The nature of the counseling will depend on the problem. Doctors may tell couples what the chances are that they will have a child with a particular genetic disorder and if treatment is available for the disease. They may advise that tests be taken by the mother early in the pregnancy, and they will ask couples for health information about their parents and other relatives.

The Human Genome Project

As soon as scientists discover specific genes and the proteins that those genes make, they can proceed to find ways to implant normal genes in people who lack them. It is estimated that there are 4,000 kinds of defective genes that cause serious hereditary disorders. So far, only about 100 of these genes have been identified, and their proteins have been decoded. But in 1990, scientists from all over the world launched a huge project to identify and decode every one of the approximately 50,000 to 100,000 human genes. This project, called the Human Genome Project, would mean that in the near future people could get a map of all of their genes.

The understanding of all human genes could yield important results. Many cures for hereditary disorders and other kinds of diseases would be possible. Other hereditary characteristics such as hair color, skin color, or body size could be changed. Some might consider this a perfect world. No one would be sick, and people could choose the way they wanted to look.

But mapping genes will also raise new questions. Should an employer be allowed to use a person's gene map to decide whether to hire that person? A gene map might reveal future illnesses that could cause that person to miss work. What about insurance companies? Should they be allowed to deny insurance to an individual because of something they find in that person's gene map? Questions like these make it clear that scientific progress causes new problems that will need to be addressed by society.

Glossary

amino acids The chemicals that make up proteins.

antibiotics Medicines that prevent or kill infection.

antibodies Proteins that defend the body against disease organisms.

autoimmune disease A disease in which the body's infection-fighting system attacks parts of the body.

birth defect A physical problem that a person is born with.

cell The basic structure that makes up all living things.

chromosome inversion The changing of the location of genes on the chromosome, which is caused by chromosome breakage.

chromosomes The tiny thread-like structures in the nucleus of each cell that contain genes.

codon Small pieces of a gene that determine the order of amino acids in proteins.

cytoplasm The area surrounding the cell's nucleus.

daughter cell One of the two cells into which a cell divides during the process of cell formation.

dominant gene One of a pair of genes that determines the effect the pair will have on the body.

egg A female sex cell.

embryo The tissue that develops into a baby.

fertilized egg An egg that has been entered by a sperm.

genes The tiny particles carried on the chromosomes of cells that make a particular protein and determine the characteristics that are passed on to children.

gene therapy The use of normal genes to treat hereditary disorders.

genetic engineering The process of inserting genes into the cells of a living organism.

hereditary disease An illness caused by a defective gene.

hormones Chemicals that regulate body processes.

Human Genome Project A scientific project that will provide a complete map of all the genes on the 23 pairs of human chromosomes.

immune system The body's defense against disease organisms.

miscarriage The loss of a developing baby.

mitochondria Hot-dog-shaped structures in the cytoplasm of cells that produce the cell's energy.

mutation A change produced in a gene.

nucleus The center of a living cell that contains the chromosomes.

ovaries The female sex glands that produce eggs.

paralysis Inability to move.

protein A chain of amino acids that plays many roles in the body.

recessive gene A gene that affects the body only if it is paired with another recessive gene.

sperm A male sex cell.

syndrome A group of symptoms that together are characteristic of a disease or condition.

testes The male sex glands that produce sperm.

virus A tiny germ that can invade cells and cause infection, and hence, disease.

X chromosome One of two chromosomes that determine a person's sex. A female has two X chromosomes. A male has an X and a Y chromosome.

X-linked disorder A hereditary disorder carried on the X chromosome.

Y chromosome One of two chromosomes that determine a person's sex. A male has one Y chromosome and one X chromosome.

Further Reading

Brown, Fern G. *Hereditary Disease*. New York: Franklin Watts, 1987.

Bryan, Jenny. *Medical Technology*. New York: Franklin Watts, 1991.

Conway, Lorraine. *Heredity & Embryology*. Carthage, IL: Good Apple, 1980.

Fekete, Irene, and Ward, Peter D. *Disease & Medicine*. New York: Facts on File, 1987.

Marshall, Eliot, and Finn, Jeffrey. *Medical Ethics*. New York: Chelsea House, 1990.

Silverstein, Alvin, and Silverstein, Virginia B. *Genes, Medicine, & You*. Hillside, NJ: Enslow Publishers, 1989.

Index

Photo Credits:
P. 4: ©Larry Mulvehill/Photo Researchers, Inc.; p. 7: ©Omikron/Science Source/Photo Researchers, Inc.; p. 8: ©Stuart Rabinowitz/Blackbirch Graphics, Inc.; p. 12: ©Andy Levin/ Photo Researchers, Inc.; p. 20: Ken Edwards/Photo Researchers, Inc.; p. 27: ©Nancy Durrell McKenna/Photo Researchers, Inc.; p. 28: ©David R. Frazier/Photo Researchers, Inc.; p. 32: ©Jackie Lewin/Royal Free Hospital/Science Photo Library/Photo Researchers, Inc.; p. 34: ©Simon Fraser/RVI, New Castle-Upon-Tyme/Science Photo Library/Photo Researchers, Inc.; p. 37: ©Martin Dohrr/Photo Researchers, Inc.; p. 40: S.I.U./Science Source/Photo Researchers, Inc.; p. 43: ©Richard Hutchings/Photo Researchers, Inc.; p. 44: ©John Watney/Photo Researchers, Inc.; p. 47: ©J. Da Cunha/Petit/Photo Researchers, Inc.; p. 50: Petit Format/Nestle/ Science Source/Photo Researchers, Inc.; p. 52: ©Lawrence Migdale/Photo Researchers, Inc.; p. 55: ©Scott Camazine/Photo Researchers, Inc.; p. 59: ©Philippe Plailly/Science Photo Library/Photo Researchers, Inc.

Technical illustrations: ©Blackbirch Graphics, Inc.